World Wildlife Alphabet

MARTHA J. WEIL

ISBN 978-1-965679-74-6 (Paperback)
ISBN 978-1-965679-75-3 (Ebook)

Inquiries and Book Orders should be addressed to:

Leavitt Peak Press
17901 Pioneer Blvd Ste L #298, Artesia, California 90701
Phone #: 2092191548

A a

Arctic wolf

B b

buffalo

C c

cockatoo

D d

dolphin

E e

elephant

F f

fruit bat

Gg

gorilla

Hh

horse

I i

impala

J j

jaguar

K k

koala bear

L 1

lemur

Mm

monarch butterfly

N n

newt

Oo

orca

P p

panda bear

Qq

quetzal

R r

rabbit

S s

snake

T t

tiger

U u

urchin

V v

vulture

Ww

wombat

X x

xantis yak

Y y

yellow-bellied sapsucker

Z z

zebra

www.ingramcontent.com/pod-product-compliance
Lightning Source LLC
Chambersburg PA
CBHW042345030426
42335CB00030B/3460